Becoming Unbroken

This journey of becoming
my choices in a tension
breaking what I was
building who I become

Samuel L. Field

First published 2020 by YndFwd

www.yndfwd.com/publishing

www.samuelfield.com

Copyright © Samuel L. Field 2020
The moral rights of the author have been asserted.

All rights reserved. No part of this book may be reproduced or transmitted by any persons or entity, in any form or by any means, electronic or mechanical, including photocopying, recording, scanning, or by any information storage and retrieval system, without prior permission in writing from the publisher.

Cataloguing-in-Publication entry is available
from the National Library of Australia
http://catalogue.nla.gov.au

This is a work of personal expression,

it reflects the authors feelings and

may not reflect others perspective and intent

Contents

Growth is 4

My Limits 18

Rest 32

Start to live 44

Let go 58

Path 68

Free to be 78

Locations & Artists 96

Author 98

For me to change
I need reasons
Often they are pain

Pain isn't chosen
Growth is

Trauma

There is no polishing
or framing it nice to tell
Anyone who lived through trauma
and will really talk about it
Describes their time in hell

Trauma is shit, it stinks, sickens and sticks. Sometimes you get a little, and with a bit of help you get past it and free, sometimes it buries people. They will never be unburdened.

Losing an arm, a leg or your sense of self in a dark night from hell. Some trauma cannot be undone long after the cause has gone. Limbs do not regrow. Your mind has parts that are just so. A burned sense of self can be damage so grave, the self may never again be complete.

Pause pain

It's so sharp, it couldn't hurt more?
Just through the thin skin on my arm
Letting some blood out, to slowly run free
Would my inner pain be stemmed, even released?

My purpose isn't more pain or death
But could blood replace tears?
Some new ways to cry
So tired are these eyes

Hurt is so deep, I don't know how to let it out
So sharp, I don't know how to numb it
Yet so much is fucking dull inside
Just this pain is clear

Pain is dirt churning in my waters of life
Dirty pain is all I can see in me
Muddied all views I find
Clouding my insight

Quiet I must be
To let my waters sleep
Allowing dirty pain to settle
Leaving calm, to see the rest of me

To death do we pause

Death takes days
Some surrendering daily
An inevitability creeping along
Moments passively passed to incineration
The wells of life's hope, gradually sand filled
Leaving scorched earth dreams behind
No hope rises from such dry places
Gentle growth is unknown
Limp, lifeless, passive
Passivity buries
Slow death
Bit by bit
Pausing
Dying

Today
I choose
To do anything
Something more
Than just laying down
As I keep doing new things
I find ways from the dying place
Turning from passivity more each day
I build new life, in places death slowly claimed

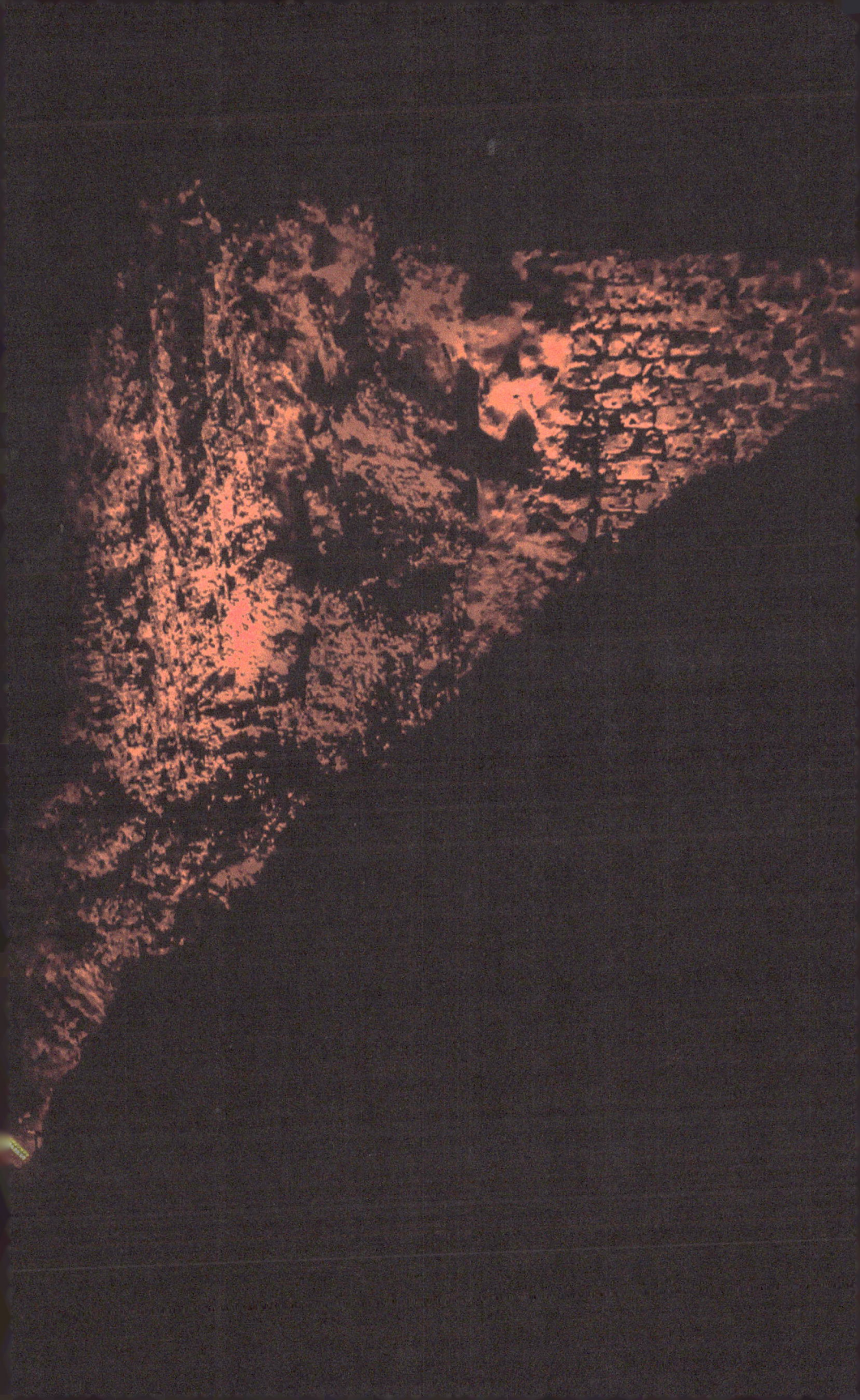

The deep calls

Void pulled at my soul, my deep
All around me is torched
Burned to nothing
I am on its edge

Looking at no surroundings
I could not stand the destruction
I could not yield to be destroyed
Yet it beckoned my surrender

The void whispered to the soul
Go down to quiet depths
Gently, let a fall take me
Do not fight, do not resist

Within I quaked between
Strength or collapse
Hopes weak vestige fading
Refuse to hold, let go?

Barely standing this pull
Quaking begat shaking
My body yearned its rest
Soul grasping for life

Pain pulled at my chest
My spirit eyed freedom
My mind numbed
No words left

I did what I couldn't
Not making a noise
My spirit cried out
I stood, Not falling

Subsided, did that urge to go
To run from this moment
From harsh reality
I stood

Then I saw new paths
Maybe nothing is there
Maybe good futures ahead
But I sense hopes cool return

Just a wet pillow?

Memories weigh my heart down but this bed is restless
I keep peering memories for understanding
This pillow wet and uncomfortable
As I rend my mind yet again

Thoughts echoing bell swings inside
Disturbing peace I wasn't feeling
My soul wants answers
But I withstood me

Anchored fast to my lack of understanding
My pillow, a wet insubstantial solace
My heart finding not the rest I seek
My mind will not wander

I plead with myself
Let me be, let me rest
Peace be mine, I want to sleep
I gave and got no peace bringing answer

The night is quiet
My crying is weak
The cold bit and held
Till dawn warmed

Modern slaves

Almost everyone I know
Owes for what they have
Friends on carers benefit
CEO's, investors, me

I don't pay it forward
I keep paying it all back
Hoping one day, if I keep earning
I can level up, earn freedom, within the game

Debt makes indebted employees
Better than indentured slaves
Is indebted the new indentured
Regardless, we keep playing

Life stilled
Dreams buffering
Passions quiet to a hum
The cloud slowly passing overhead
Floating by on a soft blue-grey screen
Distant, untouchable and disconnected
My yearnings for change have drained
Passions crowded to tiny death yelps
As I swapped my real dreams
For pretend peace

My Limits

Next steps

Tired of trying
Tired of almost there
Tired of carrying damage
Done by someone else

Some days I claw myself up
Over a boulder to discover
Twelve more ahead
Short changing hope's expectations

I feel I know where to go
Or at least I think I know the way
Finding a little resolve
I climb another boulder today

I am getting nearer my goal
Thinking of it, I feel drained
Can I find a second wind
Or will I collapse

I've never been weaker
I've never been more committed
I've never been emptier
Never had more need to keep going

Judge free me

Is death perfection?
It makes some sense
No one to disappoint

I'd make no missteps or errors
Would that not be perfection,
It would be just a loss of life

I live, somehow I fail
I try to hurt no one
but I breathe, I offend

How do I quiet these judges?
The ones you spoke to me
Inconsistent rules that confuse

Life is more then pretend perfection
In just avoiding perceived failure
Had I been living?

I won't carry judgments
For actions you didn't like
Their weight drains my life

Almost out of my head

Scenes' light invades
My inner room
A view of life beyond
Projected into head space

Bright, warm out there
This inner world is colder
Isolated air-conditioned core
Heart chilled by disconnect

Almost connecting
Life is right there
Outside my eyes
I am so close

But I just view
I dare not share
Staying trapped inside
Stuck in my own head

Fix my child

My son stayed on the ward called 4h
In the children's hospital named for a princess
The hospital is now gone like the hope it promised

I'll not forget the head psych
He tried so hard to put it gently
He couldn't soften it, it's my son

No doubts had he
He was so confident
My son couldn't be made right

No one has what it takes
My efforts were in vain
Lower my hope with pain

I can't raise him myself
I can't bring him home
I can't fix my child
I can't hold hope

Ten years past
Since that dark day
When the air drained of hope

Today he has grown
Earned a diploma
He's still at home

Orion's belt

In my spa
Smoking a cigar
Head of ideas
That go so far

Orion's belt not to far
Or so ancients felt
But now I know
They are distant stars

I'm knowing more
Thoughts expanding
But unchanged I am?
From thinkers before

Truth it seems
Always in front of all
Resting there, to be seen
With some perspective

I think I see
Then drawing
In measures
Familiar to me

Truth be fixed
My knowledge is not
Without me, truth persists
But my perspective does not

Plumbing depths of
Semi-fluid perspectives
Seeking to mine truths
That in reality rest

Know then be

I am one, but not always as one
I see things but not truly knowing
Though nothing stops me knowing
Then sometimes I know but not see

Then I can know, yet not feel it
Or feel what I do not know
How do I know, feel, or see?
Or some lesser set of these

With clarity in mind, some knowledge arrives
Then to experience, I must get free from pasts' binds
Seeing meaning, yet grasping only what I knew before
Then see, but hold only my old, not my future?
I seek freedom to see, know and feel, then be

Perception, experience, meaning, not fickle things
Try holding in the mind and letting heart sing
Equations with multiple answering
Freewill this complicated thing

Some things I see pertain to destiny
Is it my lot to see and wait to be?
Or not to see, but know then be?
Oh will you open this to me!

Sand pouring through my fingers
Yet try telling it to stay and not go
Things I see, feel and know and not be
I must keep exploring, till I choose to be

I want some rest
Time and space to de-stress
Releasing a version of my story
The one I have been driving through
I'll share some wine
Relaxing with you
Closing act two

Rest

Flowers don't bloom all year
nor moon shine at all times
The ocean surges
as the land rests

After paths end

Bonds of love and safety, destroyed
Beliefs, friendships, security
So much I rested in,
Trusted in,
Gone

From my tightly held dreams
Hope has drained
Legs walk nowhere
Direction-less wheels
Turning to where?
What purpose?

Outside was gone
I had to go in me
The deep is alive
This journey's fabric
Richer as you go slower

Crippled legs beneath me
My grounded body lay
I didn't choose this rest
Pink flowers before me
My heart rises fragrantly

Beauty infuses in destruction
My new first sight of world
The fire has cleared a way

Game over

I hear a voice calling
Calling me home
The game is over
It's time to rest

Mum at 6
Calling me in
As this day is done
Dinner will be nice

More days ahead
to practice again
So rest I will
Then win

I don't fear
My journey isn't ending
Relax with me
Accept rest

Escaping storm

My heart in a storm
My mind tries to outrun
Burning energies fleeing
Flight clearly isn't won

Turmoil without
Stirring up pain within
Memories displaced
Now along pulses race

Storm deeply embraced
Naming this, identifying
What I'm trying to flee
I learn to ride gently

My heart can calm
My boat will float
Myself, I will be
The storm is me

4 am

4am, go away

Please don't stay
Passing each night
I don't need to see you
With me awake every day

Of my many thoughts
Worries and memories
I choose them to wait
Till later today

I'd rather sleep
Than lay awake with you
Thinking things another time through
So again,

4am, go away

Passing

It will pass
Like that hangover
A wild storms fright
My babies pained cry
4am cold of night

This too will pass
Sun will come back
Hope fires anew

I will too

Start to live

Finding myself in a floor-less fall
A soul-less drone
Patently wimpy

Suddenly at a level of sorts
Picking me up, washing
Stepping outside

Breathing deeper
Starting to live again
Heart beating hope

Writing, moving
Sleep deeper
Climb

Life is for living

Dwarfed

Why should I change for them?
I will bunker, all will adjust
Their storms will just pass by

I could enjoy the sun
Bake like a rock in warmth
Unmoved by all their windy noise

As time passes I won't change
Just some seasonal wear
My rock self changes not

Not like the gumtree I sit under
Its top most branch
Broken in a storm

I've seen this tree in glory
Enjoyed its former full canopy
Even tried to climb, when it was smaller

Despite storm weathered damage
This broken and growing tree
Still dwarfs me

Positive denial

I decided not to be real for them
To be only as they expected
Hiding my parts unique

Death is an absence of life
But Life is not death's absence
I shallowed my life, not full of me
I traveled a partial road to slow death

NO MORE! I will show up as myself
Not in costumes left from before
Distorting mE to fit within
As I am, I must be

I seek THIS! life
Abounding in realness
Denying death and fear
Compounding victories

See the end

Thoughts rushing my awareness
Pointless reminders, concern sharpened
Distractions startling then stopping me
Are these my thoughts and not my choice?

Incrementally I lined up these thoughts
My concentration, I had to force
Wrestling this mind into focus
So much rattling in there

I am pushing that extra mile
In this long distance race
Feeling drained, done
More pool laps to do

I am determined to be
My belief underpins
Actions forming
My character

The mettle of me
My real backbone
Will I push when grit-
dust is all I have?

Social rules allow, permit me to collapse
It is acceptable, expected to cease
I hear my own voice within
I will see the end of this!

Flaming play-dough

Need my fire die
Passion recede to sea
or can I keep breaking
on beaches of change, adaptability

Am I like play-dough?
Soft and mold-ably young
Brittle, unbendable as time passes
A limited useful window of life

Did adapting leave me dry?
Am I only useful for a while
Or am I stifling life within
Shaped by expectations

Do I have to risk again?
Evermore breaking molds
So let the curtain lower
To rise on a new line

Is the dice limited in throws?
Yes but! Sixes do come
I'll throw with hope
Roll that dice

Life on the shelf dries first
Play-dough gets oil
From play
PLAY!

Buried

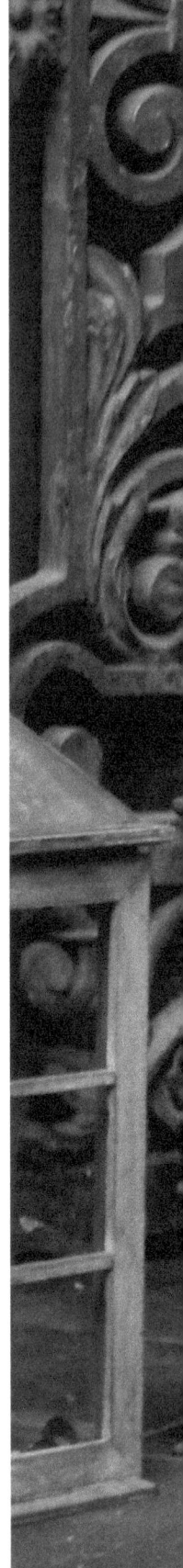

Some of the biggest fires
start not with a spark
but smoldering
under layers
across years

Climb?

Are there no other ways but hard ones?
Walk on, climb higher, I bear me
or what else should I do?
Lay down, shrink
atrophy

Not me
I carry me on
To a barely seen future
Walking, climbing or even crawling
I will find resolve, building strength once more

Let go

I cannot be
All that I was
As I am becoming
All I am choosing to be

Free is within

Reaching the end of what I control
Trying to make the world work
According to what I want
My speed, My way

Striving died a little tonight
As I laid my head to rest
My eyelids lowered
Breathing slowed

Circulating 'driven thoughts'
Leaving me, as I let go
of what I do not
can not control

Others and Outcomes
Not mine to own
I am my own

My energy's not to be changing out
It will be on changing in
The me that is free

No more

Pain and loss?
No more suffering
No more heart held
In agonies wrenching hand
I'm done blinking away tears
Through years

I paused at pain

Again, pain, I push away
In pushing, I had to touch
Burning my heart each time
On memories I hadn't let fade

Stalled in my return to pain
My deepest soul, shut down
Heart jammed on the past
I cannot just...move on

I've felt some go
Long strings plied out
Step by step, I let pieces go
Untangling such mess, entwined

Locked up threads to undo
Some can be ripped
But pain in each
Handling too

In pausing,
I prolonged no fun
I kept stalling...letting pain
Stay for too long

A long carriage

I have carried long enough
Words not my own
Under their weight
Rejections of me
I part broke

Pondering suffers me
For hurting to cease
I chose to release
I stop grasping at
'Why your rejection'

I choose to not self remind
That you didn't see me
Even if no one else
I choose to see
I am enough

.....I'm not blind
But I don't always see

So when it's clear
I choose to commit
To memory

Path

Avoiding my wine

I didn't want to drink my memories
I sipped and spat,
By their potent smell, I put me off
Why should I want, what you had rejected

I pushed me away
In order to swap drinks
To try or be something else
Instead of what I had been

Down went distracting vodka
On went music cooler than I am
Switching to Gin that others clearly liked
Perhaps I could share their identity

Over, again and again
I drank more than my fill
New distractions each time
But my drink, sat there still

I drank till I puked and stank
But not of me
I had exhausted my drive
Yet I had avoided me still

Behold memories stored and bottled
After my ignoring, still there
But I was done, I was shot
I nor they, were going anywhere

Facing such a full bottle
Seeing me pushed away
I had put so much there
My shell nearly emptied

I started to sip
A bitter start, then sweet
Part heavy, then surprisingly light
This aged self wine

I drank more as I could
I felt energy and gained insight
Familiar tastes, more understood
It was slow and it was healing

Slowly drinking my life's wine
Sweet highs and deep lows
My fruits and my tannins
Poured back in this clay vessel

This journey, it is mine
It could not be so let go
I value my own true self
It is the only vine I can grow

Growing curious

I am living to see tomorrow
Can I handle more?
How will I grow?
What it will be like?
These futures unknown

But, when hope dives
I lose drive
Not curious
Dreading tomorrow
Risk facing fears deeply known

Imagine knowing
Every future detail
As the past is known
Would I feel like re-living
What's already known?

So I'll hold out and hold on
To hope with tomorrow
Let new days come
I'll stay curious to grow

Path seen

I saw it all so clearly
How it all fits
What to do

Its fading
I'm questioning
I thought I knew

Passing light
This briefest flash
Illuminated my path

As a flash in a fire
Quick as storms thunder
Glimpse from lightning

A brief encounter
Throwing my sight
Might make my life

I took stock
I knew where to go
Now to trust myself

Lit sojourn

Starting on a path I don't know
The known is gone, so new it is
Though it's an obscured view
A light ahead I perceive

It seems so far
Towards that light
Steps I keep choosing
By hopes of mine

It's a dim lit sojourn
I'll not stay here, I can't
So I'm headed through
On a vaguely lit path

Tired as I truly am
I have nearly crossed
Todays' bridge I found
I'm closer to a new life

Free to be

Don't hold me down
Or hold me back
What I will be
Let me choose
And I will be
Every day

Beautiful echo

They put bounds on my speech
Stories they didn't want told
To be among, I must conform
Not to say my world as I see it

But isn't freedom?
Hearing my own voice
Freedom from being
Bound till silent

They needed to hear me
to give me space in their world
instead I needed to hear me
then I was free

I chose to leave, they locked the door
They wanted me gone by then
My voice wouldn't conform
It never would again

Peace, meaning and surprise joy
Freedom in my own voice
Hearing my own sounds
My echo is beautiful

I Lied

I am not the things I tell myself
Kind
Honest
True too

I lie to me
I lied to you
I said this shit
I thought it too

I'm better than all
That's pride, no way
Cause I'm more humble
And much cleverer instead

I am not the things I tell myself
Kind, honest and true, I lied to you
So I might believe I wasn't lying
To me too

Meaningful pursuit

Freedom cost is vigilance
Attending its many calls
Equality its high aim
Self determination for all

It is never achieved!
This unreachable goal
But with intent, energy
Clear pursuit on-goes

This pursuit has meaning
Deep truths unfolding
When we cease attention
Are truths learned hard

Stained Heart

My inner world
turned to gray
covered in ash
from what I was
with tears I cried
as I lost parts of me

I write a new world
Ideas of what will be
taking what remained
my heart staining
this inner world
in hopes colours

Colour me in

Life
Squiggles
Many major lines
Like a child's drawing
Are a given on our pages
The colours are yours
You choose?

Lifting hope

I woke before dawn
My journey, its concerns, fluxing
Running in a tumble through this head
So I walked me and them out the front door

Contemplating what to do
How tangled these concerns
Where can I find a happy end
Or a just conclusion

Peering towards dawn's sharp arrival
Light spilling horizon's brim
Yellows pouncing gray earth
Shadows leaping grass blades in turns

The settled dew starts to lift
Hope hangs above the ground
Glistening from warming rays
Sunlight kicks off this new day

Choosing to be naked

I saw into my heart
a mixture of pride and shame
I accept my inner soul
yet choose not to remain the same

I face my spirit forward
I'm letting go
Of who I was
I celebrate the deepest part of me

Living in this tension
Between who I was
And who I Am
I choose me

Rise

With the rain on desert plains
Moisture brought to ground
Seeds open to life

Rising so quickly
Small forests of life
Desert was just containing

I did not surrender to death
And with new rain
I will rise

 Como Beach Jetty – Como

 Farm house balcony – York

 The Tav – Curtin University

 Hayman Theatre – Curtin University

 Rooftop – Northbridge

 Atkinson Forum – Curtin University

 Scouts Jetty – South Perth

 Como Beach Jetty – Como

 Karma – Rottnest Island

 Dead Wood – Collins Pool

 Church – A Country Town in WA

 Streeter's Jetty – Broome

 Arthur Head – Fremantle

 Coopers Mill – Cooleenup Island

 Olive Farm – York

 Beach – Myalup

 "Maralinga" by Lin Onus 1990 – Art Gallery WA

 Rooftop Bar – Melbourne Victoria

 Night – South Perth

 Milky Way – Yeagarup

 Kings Carnival – Mandurah

 Mangrove Hotel – Broome

 Coopers Mill – Cooleenup Island

Thrombolites – Lake Clifton

Street Art
–Fremantle

"to the Fishermen"
by Jon Tarry & Greg James
–Fremantle

A Balcony
–Perth

Restaurant
–Melbourne, Vic

One Way Sign
–Fremantle

Southgate
–Melbourne

Hotel, Melbourne

Path behind me
–Preston Beach

Yeagarup Dunes
–Pemberton

Farm
–York

Gantheaume Point Rocks
–Broome

Como Beach Jetty
–Como

By door
–Melbourne

Peaceful Bird
–Como

Pinnacles Desert
–Namburg National Park

Hyatt Regency Lobby
–Denver, Colorado

View atop Kings Park
–Perth

Street Art
–Subiaco

Seat & Path
–Rockingham, WA

Overpass
–Como

Outside
–Fremantle

View from Jetty
–Como

Farm
–York

On Way
–Fremantle

Pages stained with more
Than words, black ink and colour
Layers, fragments, pieces of self
Crossing into photographs
All of me and not of all
So here's one more both
The same, yet it's not

Story uniquely me
Reflections of you here
Shared experiences found
Our journeys do overlap
Sameness, difference
We share waves

www.ingramcontent.com/pod-product-compliance
Lightning Source LLC
Chambersburg PA
CBHW040243010526
44107CB00065B/2856